Dedicated to all the kids who were bullied.

Taylor Walker

The Lone Wolf © Taylor Walker 2014
ISBN 978-1-4951-1947-7

Once upon a time, there was a small playful wolf. He had orange fur with green eyes.

He was often bullied by other wolves.
One day he and his pack went out hunting.

5

He found a stick, and he played with the stick.
The pack went off without him.

7

When he soon realized that the pack had gone without him, he howled to tell them that they had left him behind. But there was no response.

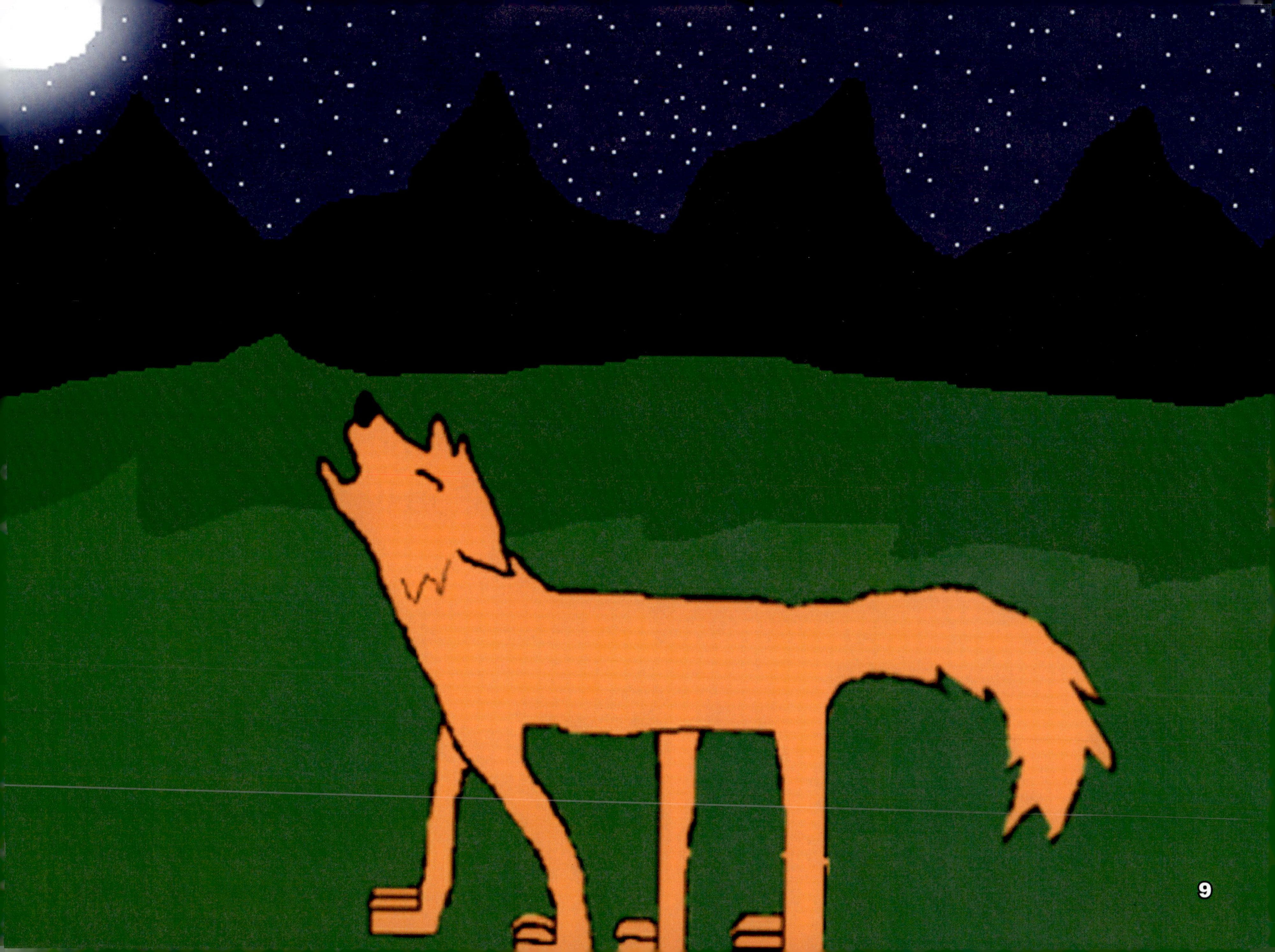

He was lost for two days, hungry and cold. But then a wolf from his pack ran up to him with tears in her eyes. She said she was sorry for bullying him and leaving him there.

11

He forgave her, and he asked her if she wanted to join his pack. She said yes, and they asked other lone wolves to join their pack.

13

One day the little pack was digging a hole for a den that would keep them warm in the winter.

15

But then the orange wolf's old alpha came to their den and growled at them to leave. The small pack didn't listen, so the old alpha called his big pack forward and growled at them to leave.

17

The small pack gathered together and howled. A storm started and a crackle of lightning struck near the old alpha. The old alpha was so scared that he ran off with his pack.

19

After that, their pack grew into a big pack. They had a pup, and they lived...

21

happily ever after.

The End

23